Journey of a Broken Seeker

What readers say…

"There is something about your writing that breathes life into my soul and lifts my spirit. That awakens me to the glorious beauty of this world and the depth of God's love for us. I identified with so much. Thank you for your vulnerability that allows me to say, "oh yes, me too!" and for the hope that your writing gives."

"I fell in love with your book on the first line. I also found many bits really touched me and moved me. It has counselled me and blessed me. Thank you. To quote you, Don't stop."

"I am so so blessed by reading this and I know I will return to it again and again. Thank you for putting the words down! They are life giving, affirming, instructional, and most of all loving. I am really encouraged and moved in reading this."

Journey of a Broken Seeker

one woman's search for the Heart of God

a seeker's heart: book 1

B. Belinda Strotheide

Copyright © 2021 B. Belinda Strotheide

All rights reserved. No part of this book may be reproduced or used in any manner without written permission of the copyright owner, except for the use of brief quotations in a book review.

To request permissions, contact:
support@seedstockmedia.com

Paperback: ISBN 978-0-9970170-3-8
First paperback edition October 2021

Front cover image by B.B. Strotheide

Unless otherwise noted, all Scripture quotations are from the ESV® Bible (The Holy Bible, English Standard Version®), copyright © 2001 by Crossway Bibles, a publishing ministry of Good News Publishers. Used by permission.
All rights reserved.

Seed Stock Press
PO Box 132207
Tyler, TX 75713-2207

www.seedstockpress.com

DEDICATION

To my parents, Charles and Vickie Traver, whose prayers are most likely the reason I found my way home to God.

To my husband, Mike, who has always made a safe place for me to write and create and supported me through it all.

TABLE OF CONTENTS

Introduction	1
1 The Invitation	5
2 The Quest	15
3 The Call	27
4 The Road	45
5 The Heart of God	67
About the Author	91
Thank You	93

Introduction

"If we find ourselves with a desire that
nothing in this world can satisfy,
the most probable explanation is that
we were made for another world."

C. S. Lewis

I wanted to be friends with the God who created giraffes and elephants. I longed to know the Creator of night skies, nebula, and mysterious ocean creatures. I wanted to meet George Washington Carver's[1] God of the unfolding peanut mysteries. The God who conceived the idea of seeds. The One who dreamed up colors and music.

I was not looking for a religion. I was seeking a connection to the Creator of the aardvark, the iris, and the butterfly. I was hungry for life. A rich, full life that was bigger than my pain, my doubt, and darkness. I found the words of religion heavy to carry. Confining. And many times, filled with fear and warning. Weighing me down in winter clothes in the midst of summer. I learned to see beauty in religious rituals, but they were never my first activity when seeking God. Sitting in the dirt watching wildflowers dance in a summer breeze was where I saw Him.

---

[1] GW Carver researched plants and flowers and sought God to find mysteries in creation. He's one of America's greatest inventors, a pioneering agriculturalist, award-winning artist, and humble man of faith. www.tinyurl.com/CarverArticle

Sometimes when we hurt, our focus becomes limited to avoiding pain. That was true for me. I spent a lifetime developing methods to keep people out of my personal life. Techniques to guard my heart against the wounding of others. Trust doesn't come easily to the broken. It required so much energy to feel safe. Then one day, when I was tired of doing life my way and still not feeling protected, I heard God say, "Take down your walls, Dear One. I want to come in and be friends with you."

I wrestled with His words, believing He might be part of the problem, but when I said yes, even though I didn't really trust Him; when I stood believing still in my own independence and angry to the core at injustice and unmet needs, Jesus came into my heart. He stepped right past the anger to the center of it all. To the pain that leaked like toxic waste, corroding everything within me and dripping out of my mouth. He wrapped His arms around my wounded child-heart and in some mysterious way healed me with His love. With the healing came a desire and power to forgive, to bless those who hurt me, and to repent of my own stubbornness of holding onto grudges and bitterness.

Like the water within my cells calls out to the water in a running river or mountain lake, so the spirit within me has always cried out for the Spirit of God. Until I met Jesus, there was only the dream of being filled, only the torment of being broken and empty.

1 The Invitation

What do you think? If a man has a hundred sheep, and one of them has gone astray, does he not leave the ninety-nine on the mountains and go in search of the one that went astray?

Matthew 18:12

The Invitation

For most of my life, my spiritual walk was not anything I wanted to share because it was so uncomfortable. I longed for a relationship with God, but was afraid of Him. Leaning forward while backing away. Why would I invite others into a way of living that seemed a bit tormented? Believing there was a God who was, in fact, real but not understanding Him enough to see an impact? I was hungry for a spiritual life but saw only bits and pieces, nothing large or meaningful enough to fill or heal. How could I, in good conscience, offer this to others? My short answer: I couldn't. And never really did. It's not that I was ashamed of God, just wary, fearful, and definitely not a credible witness of His goodness. I lived trapped in a space just short of the promised land, looking longingly toward a place of freedom and joy.

Who takes our hands and leads us alongside Jesus so we might look into His face and see only love? People like Heidi Baker[2] kept me seeking, asking, knocking, and hoping for a personal glimpse

---

[2] Heidi Baker is a missionary in Mozambique and president of Iris ministries where they are "Compelled by the love of God to stop for the one in need." www.irisglobal.org

of His goodness as she expressed through her ministry.

She went after the one. The one lost in the darkness of a poverty-stricken nation. Jesus walked with her into the village right to the one who was most without hope. The one woman there who had such little value, she had never even been given a name.

Jesus left the ninety-nine sheep to go after the one who was lost. That is the Jesus I was desperate to know. The Jesus who placed such a high value on me He left Heaven to bring me life. He actually died to give me an introduction to my Heavenly Father. Died so I could be loved deeply and extravagantly. So I could know my Father who created wildflowers, whales, rivers, and summer skies for me.

Invitations to the Unseen

God was always real to me. When I was around four years old, I sensed His presence watching over me. When I was six, I learned about Jesus and Hell in Sunday School. Convinced I wanted no part of fiery torment, I accepted Jesus into my heart. Sadly, I remembered the images of eternal damnation much more vividly than those of the love of God.

Back then, the unseen realm pushed into my life in ways that mostly brought distress. I had nightmares of the Indiana Jones variety. Recurring, complete with snakes and spiders. As a visually sensitive child, the movie Bambi was disturbing, and I began to have recurring nightmares of fire, too. When I was nine, I saw a fireball crash from the sky. No one else saw it. The entire family came outside with me to find evidence of it. But nothing was there.

That was one of many experiences that were unexplainable, but very real to me. I learned then that most people don't believe in anything they don't see, so I wandered in and out of the supernatural pretty much alone. I didn't share those experiences and, until now, have told only a few close friends.

I have come to believe that all the supernatural experiences I had were simply invitations from God. Invitations to come closer. To seek who He is and how He thinks. To understand how He loves and how He wants to be with me.

In dreams, I have been given things I don't understand. Scepters, robes, oranges. I see pictures when I pray and God unfolds the stories and their meanings as I wait on Him. Once, while praying, I saw myself as a little girl playing in a forest, creating a small garden from flowers, twigs, and stones. Out of nowhere, a large rock settled in my hand. I wondered about it and then looked around for something to do with it. I pounded it on the side of a tree. I drug it through the dirt in my garden making a ditch. I played catch with it. As I reached my arm back to give it a good throw, I felt Jesus behind me. He gently took the rock and broke it into two pieces. Inside were the most lovely crystals, brightly purple and reflecting light in every direction. Jesus set the pieces in my garden, moving them with precision to a specific place at the foot of a flower, then He turned and smiled and held out His hand.

From this story, I learned that when God gives me gifts, I probably won't know what they're for. His gifts, like dreams and supernatural encounters, are invitations to a conversation. To ask Him what they mean or what to do with them. Where to use them. How to make them work. Like parents give a child an activity set to play with their young son or daughter, so God gives gifts to connect with us. To spend time with us. To love and be loved by His children.

I discovered there are invitations everywhere to conversations with God. He is hungry to talk to us, to be friends, and enjoy time with us. I noticed that so many times when He gives me a gift, a dream, or an idea, I just take it and run off with it. Sometimes I don't even say, "Thank You." But since the garden story, I've realized He gives gifts so He can connect with me. Giving splendid gifts in hopes I will turn to Him and ask Him to participate.

He is mysterious, surprising, and beautiful. There are so many things He's given me in the past that I never asked Him about. I wonder why it took me so long to understand He wants to share Himself with me. To see His whole intent in sending Jesus was to have a relationship with me.

Our Heavenly Father loves us so deeply, yet we may not recognize His invitations to come closer. Sometimes we automatically head to the library, church, or our spiritual friends when we're given a heavenly gift. Conferring with others, first. Seeking their knowledge of the usefulness and explanation of the gift. Their perception of its value.

Perhaps the gift is simply an invitation to come visit The One who adores us. Perhaps its work is to invite us to see The One who delights in being with us. Perhaps it is only for beautifying a garden, not building roads or defeating foes. Or perhaps it is Jesus' way of tossing rocks at our windows and inviting us out to play.

The Invitation

My Prayer

Heavenly Father, help me to be sensitive to your invitations. Help me to see what you've put in my life that points to you.

Open the eyes of my heart, Lord, so I can connect with your love. I want to have more conversations with you. I want to hear your plans and dreams for me and the purpose for the gifts you've given me.

Thank you for hearing my prayers and answering the cry of my heart. I pray this in Jesus' name, amen.

You have said, "Seek my face."
My heart says to you,
"Your face, Lord, do I seek."

Psalm 27:8

One thing have I desired of the LORD, that will I seek after; that I may dwell in the house of the LORD all the days of my life, to behold the beauty of the LORD, and to inquire in his temple.
Psalm 27:4

2 The Quest

"In the cave you fear to enter
lies the treasure that you seek."

Joseph Campbell

The Quest

> You will seek me and find me
> when you seek me with all your heart.
> Jeremiah 29:13

I had a dream a few years ago where I was traveling from church to church, searching through their teachings and books, eagerly seeking truth. Finally, after I had been at this for some time, Jesus showed up. He stood in front of me as if to ask what I was doing. His face was so bright. He didn't speak out loud, but into my heart, saying, "I am who you seek. I am the message. Seek me."

My true spiritual quest started not so long ago when I realized I did not love God with my whole heart. Something in me resisted Him. Some distrust lived in a dark corner of my heart. A belief that if I gave God all of me my worst fears would be realized. He would not be a good Father but a terrorizing ruler. One who would see my shortcomings, my lack, my sin, and banish me from His kingdom.

What lies the enemy of God wraps around us. Like a kitten unraveling a ball of string, I followed the lie until it entangled me completely. Until it immobilized me spiritually with a deep foreboding of who God really was and what He wanted with me.

"In the cave you fear to enter lies the treasure that you seek."

This quote was on my wall for over a year while a loving God gently spoke words of truth and kindness to my shaking, broken, child-heart that was desperately afraid of the dark. He spoke until I understood the depth of His goodness. The extravagance of His love. Until I became brave enough to invite Him into the darkness of my heart. Until I was able to ask Him why I resisted Him and to help me give Him my whole heart.

Seeking allowed me to see His compassion and kind intentions toward me. I am loved beyond my imagination's ability to understand. A world created in beauty, in wonder... for me. A beloved, only Son, given in pain and death... for me, so my Heavenly Father could meet with me face to face. I discovered His heart longs to be loved by me. By His children. We will never be home until we seek Him beyond the fear into the cave of the unknown. This is faith. This is seeking.

Let Him lead you into the place of unknown. Seek Him and you will find His Father's heart that delights in you. When God formed His biggest dream, He created you and me. He created an amazing earth, a lovely garden for us. To show us what He is like. To show us how He loves in extravagance and beauty. His love is truly never-ending, but to find it, to find Him, we must look up from our busy tasks and intentionally look for Him. He has promised to be found when we seek. He wants us to find Him.

> ... from there you will seek the Lord your God and you will find him, if you search after him with all your heart and with all your soul.
>
> Deuteronomy 4:29

How to See

God continues to speak softly to me. Sometimes in the whisper of a butterfly dance–so quickly, so quietly. If I'm not listening, I miss the sound. He has always been that way with me. I've never had breathtaking visions or the overwhelming arrival of Jesus or angels in the middle of the night.

Occasionally, when I lift my eyes to Heaven, I think about what it would be like to see a burning bush or wrestle with an angel. But mostly I enjoy the simple, subtle way He speaks to me, and appreciate the part of His personality He planted in my heart. The part that sees and hears gently.

Slamming doors and angry voices echo harshly through my body. I've always had a physical reaction to decibels. There is pain in my bones at loud concerts. I cannot go to places of great noise. This characteristic is not a condition to be fixed. It is not part of my brokenness. It is part of my Father's heart showing up in me. To fulfill my perfect design, I need to learn the dance of butterfly wings.

My high school science teacher taught his students observation skills. He sent us out to stake off a small plot of ground somewhere in our world and to observe it. We were assigned to record what we saw and told to describe it. How tall was the grass from week to week? What color was the dirt? What kind of animals came and went? How many types of plants grew in our little corner?

For months, I sat in my spot and watched the grass grow. I saw changes in the color of the weeds and observed the activities of several small creatures. I noticed subtle changes that intrigued me. That stirred my curiosity about creation and the colorful world around me.

Not until ten years later did I hear another person speak about observation skills. An art professor connected me to a visual encounter with the surrounding environment. She taught me how to express that experience using a variety of media. I learned intentional focus, and it was focus that allowed me to see God interrupting my physical reality. Focus helped me notice the delicate dance of butterflies. This awareness I have, this wonder and sensitivity to the lovely things surrounding me, is a part of my personality that delights God.

Sometimes I see how out of step I am with the world. I feel the roar of a passing jet, its wings loud and painful, yet pulling me along. I feel the rushing speed of my busy life. Running so fast, I don't notice butterflies or see them dance. But I, and you, are designed to observe. To experience subtle songs and beauty for each one of us to explore. Choreographed by The One who loves us best. Something uniquely You is hidden in plain sight while He waits for you to discover it. While He waits for you to hear Him calling. Hear Him singing over you.

How to Seek

How do you seek the Lord with all your heart? I know I struggle to define 'Seeking God.' What does it look like? Is it going off to a monastery in solitude and meditating quietly alone? Is that how I should separate myself as unto the Lord? As appealing as it sounds, and yes, it really does sound lovely to me, that is not what seeking at my house looks like.

It looks like getting up earlier than I want to and having a conversation with God, my Heavenly Father, who actually wants to talk to me. He doesn't always stay on my topics, but He does show up when I take time to wait. I do not wait well, but over time I've gotten better at it.

If I want to seek the Lord, I know I must create a space in my world where He is welcome. Where He can come and visit with me through His Word, through teachings, through my own prayers and worship. Can He believe I'm in with all of my heart if I don't set a time or place where He is invited to talk without distraction?

I discovered making that time for Him was one of the hardest things to do. My life was so busy, so filled with noise, work, expectations, and commitments that any extra time was a great luxury. In the beginning, I wasn't sure I wanted to spend that time on God. Horrible thing to say, but true. Surely God knew how busy I was? It felt wrong. It felt like an extravagance to sit when I should have been getting something done. Surely He understood all the things that needed to be accomplished in the next several hours. Did He really want me to sit quietly reading, praying, and listening?

Yes, He understood my work schedule and yes, He really wanted me to carve out time to be with Him. The only way to know God is to spend time with Him. Simple, right? One of the greatest fights I've ever had was to make a consistent time in my life for God. Everything, and I mean everything, opposed this effort.

I saw a picture one day while I was praying. It was a water faucet. I saw my hand turn it on when I needed the water and off when I was done. I felt the Lord's voice inside saying, "This is what life in the Kingdom of God is like." I saw that everything I needed was sourced from God. When I needed water, financial resources, emotional supply, hope, peace, or anything else that was missing, I could turn on the faucet and it would come pouring out of

Heaven. Wow. What an idea. A true image that there is no lack in God. But I didn't understand how I could access the supply.

Sometime later, while I was praying about a financial need, I heard the question, "Do you know what the handle of that faucet is?" I didn't know.

"It's stewardship," He said.

Well, there was a sinking sensation in my belly. My brain filled with thoughts of despair because I was a bad steward of money. It was always a challenge. Feast or famine was the sort of lifestyle I'd experienced as a self-employed business owner. In the middle of my chaotic thoughts, I heard Him say—and I need to tell you this is the only time in my life God has interrupted me. Usually, when I fuss about something, He simply stops talking and waits for me to be quiet. Not this time. He spoke right over my thoughts, so I knew it was important to Him and I should pay attention. He said,

"It is not stewardship of money that allows you to live resourced from My Kingdom. It is stewardship of My presence, of our relationship, that determines your connection to Heaven."

Stewarding my time with Him. Whew. I was so relieved. He had asked me to do something I knew I could do. He did not shame me for my past, but encouraged me into a future of coming closer. Of learning His heart and ways that are so different from mine. He has mysteries, opportunities, strategies to share that I will never know if I don't sit with Him and wait to hear what's on His heart and mind.

So now most mornings you will find me sitting quietly seeking, waiting, and listening. Spending the time to steward this spiritual relationship that I thought was my gift to Him, but now see it is His gift to me.

My Prayer

Heavenly Father, help me seek you. Help me find you. Help me steward a deeper relationship with you. Help me receive your love.

As Paul prayed, help me be rooted and grounded in your love, that I may understand what is the breadth and length and height and depth of it and to know the love of Christ which surpasses knowledge.

Thank you for your amazing love for me. Thank you for the gift of your presence. In Jesus' name, amen.

So God created man in his own image,
in the image of God he created him;
male and female he created them.
Genesis 1:27

3 The Call

"To send light into the darkness of men's hearts -
such is the duty of the artist."

Robert Schumann

The Call

> I praise you, for I am fearfully and
> wonderfully made. Wonderful are your
> works; my soul knows it very well.
> Psalm 139:14

You and I are created in the image of God. Made like The One who is beautiful. Which makes us beautiful, too. I think we learn what is beautiful from God. From the people and things He created. Colors, textures, shapes. Singing birds, gurgling water, crashing waves. The taste of watermelon or a crisp pepper. The smell of jasmine or gardenias on a hot summer day.

We learn about inner beauty from seeing into the hearts of people, not from looking at the external trappings of race, size, age, or cultural coverings, but seeing into hearts where dreams live, where common hopes are shimmering. Where dormant gifts lie waiting quietly for acknowledgment or permission to rise. Hearts where Jesus comes to melt walls of fear. To bring healing for brokenness and to remove slivers of unbelief, unforgiveness, and pride.

He does not judge us. He comes to heal us and to wrap us in grace and make us whole. There is beauty all around us. There is beauty within us. Beauty calls to us.

God's Heart for Beauty

My past is a trail highlighted by the places where flowers grew. I can track my life in flowers and foliage. I can't tell you who was with me during many childhood events, or even what we did, but I can tell you the colors of the flowers and the kind of plants that grew nearby.

I've always been drawn to flowers. My first wanderings, at the age of four, were in search of flowers. Out of the yard, into the nearby graveyard, and across the lawn to bouquets conveniently placed for my little fingers and sniffing nose to find. (Yes, that journey got me into trouble.) I have no memory of the gravestones but I still remember the flowers. And later there was my encounter with the iris.

It's only recently I've come to see how my path has been dusted by beauty, scents, and the colors of flowers. I denied them room in my life for many years as I sought a professional career. I was a woman in management in a man's world. Yes, it was a struggle back in those days. In one instance, I was actually told to my face I would never get the job because I wasn't a man. I met the challenges and won some battles, but the cost was high. What it really took from me was the beauty of flowers. I began to choose black or brown suits and filled my world with dark, muted colors to diminish any femininity that might come leaking out and undermine my goals. But I've come to realize flowers are part of the identity God formed in me. I was created to respond to flowers and when I don't there is something sadly missing. The color of my life becomes gray.

Flowers speak to me of many things. They artistically express beauty, color, form, and shape. I see the essence of God in the glory of a flower. They also speak to me of hope. Flowers are the evidence a plant is going to produce fruit. The sign there is something more to come. Flowers remind me of transition. A flower is only one stage in the life of a plant. A lovely one, but not the end, as there will be fruit and more seeds produced. As I contemplate a delicate bloom, I see the promise in a single flower and have hope.

One day, not so long ago, I realized I had permission to enjoy flowers. That loving them did not diminish my strength. The power of beauty superseded my perception of fragility. Just because it looked fragile didn't mean it was—not in ways that mattered. I saw that simply because a flower was delicate didn't mean it couldn't stand up to storms or burst its way through rocks to bloom on frozen mountain tops. Like love is stronger than death and nothing can stop it.

I always come back to the idea that beauty has the power to change the world. We are designed to respond to what's beautiful in nature, in people, and in relationships. We are created to resonate to music, art, poetry, and stories. Sometimes it takes discipline for me to accept the gift of flowers from God. I have to pay attention when I'm in a hurry or busy or I will miss all the flowers He's put in my path to remind me of His love and beauty. If we slow down and focus, we'll see what God puts in front of us every day to remind us of His heart.

A Beautiful Journey

It is not that my journey is always beautiful, but there are points, markers, spaces of beauty along the way. Enough to keep me seeking for more. Looking for the lovely in everyday life.

There is dangerous beauty in the night sky of ripe stars dripping to the earth in a minus 40 degree Dakota winter. A field of dangerous cold that can kill you if you breathe it in. The fearful beauty of the unknown; shimmering creatures scuttling along the ground in humid places. There is power in beauty that moves, touches, exalts, captures, surprises, and changes us. Our spirits resonate to its vibrations.

The iris was the first breathtaking moment of beauty for me. The spot in the road that changed everything in my life when I was six years old. The iris bloomed next to an old house where we recently moved. I came around the corner of the side yard and stopped. Breath caught. There it was. As tall as I was. A glorious purple iris. I reached out to touch the velvet petals. Captured by its loveliness, rich color, and grape-like smell. My first experience with the concept of elegance. The sight, touch, and smell captured and filled my young heart.

I have seen thousands of irises since that day and they still fill me with wonder, but the memory of that first one bursting into my world with its expression of beauty was special. That one iris opened my eyes to splendor and made me believe in a beautiful journey.

Momentous Beauty

The power of beauty can change the world. Smelling roses can change your life. I am convinced that focusing on beautiful things can change hearts forever. We are designed to respond to beauty. When we do not take time to see the divine beauty in creation or in each other, there is a roaring emptiness within us.

Few of us are taught to see beauty in everyday things. To really look at the materials or patterns that make up the world around us. We are mostly too busy to recognize shades of light and shadow or subtle color shifts in plants at dawn, fields in summer, or city streets during a rainstorm. Art, music, people, nature, and everyday things can all carry the lovely, the pure, and the beautiful when we take time to look.

Artists, inventors, musicians, storytellers, and all who are truly imaginative can be the most tormented in life. People born with creative souls and receptors tuned to slight nuances see and feel things in ways others do not and can suffer greatly.

The Call

We resonate when encountering beauty and truth. We are calmed by the lovely, whether words, pictures, nature, or music. There is no point in telling us to get our feelings off our sleeves because we can't. Although we can and do build walls to protect ourselves from those who enjoy poking us—people who simply have no notion of being attached to the world through color or song, but we can't turn off who we are without losing our souls.

We're like the peculiar jellyfish that washes up on a beach irresistible to curious but insensitive people passing by. The ones fearful of the unknown use sticks to jab at the quivering creature. Braver ones may use fingers to nudge the strange, shimmering mass. A beached jellyfish gets poked, prodded, and stepped on. It can even be smashed with rocks by those threatened by the mysterious.

What we don't understand makes us afraid. I know because I respond the same way to the unknown. When that large, speckled, bug-thing in Texas comes charging at me all legs, tail, and wings, I do not stop to find out if it's a beneficial bug before I start swatting away. But on certain days, I remember I am called to be creative and I see the unknown as a big playground where I let my imagination and curiosity run wild. On those days, I research bug directories in hopes I can be a better neighbor to the good but odd-looking bugs in my backyard.

A box jellyfish is pretty interesting. It can have up to 24 eyes. Real eyeballs like ours made of lenses, retinas, and corneas. That's pretty advanced for an invertebrate. These eyes are set in pairs around their bells, pointing in different directions, giving them a 360-degree view. Although this gives them the ability to detect prey, the primary purpose of these eyes is to keep them properly oriented in the water where they live. They move with beauty and intentionally focus on being in the right position in their world, which is not on land.

Their expanded sight is not given so they can focus on their enemies, which makes me think creative people are not given extra senses to fixate on the works of darkness, either. Our real calling is to explore beauty and truth and express it in a million different ways to others. So people who don't have as many eyes can see God's wonder, majesty, and love and be drawn to Him.

Jellyfish are composed of 95% water. The stuff of their true home. They are vulnerable on beaches but powerful in the vast spaces of wide, deep oceans. I believe creativity is mostly spiritual, and the ones called to it hunger for wide, deep spiritual lives. For creative souls transitioning to their true home, their genuine work, the effort begins in our hearts, not our jobs, or ministries.

Once while I worshiped, I heard God say He didn't create me to build businesses. I was so excited. For years, I wanted to live a creative life rather than build a business. I thought He had given me permission to quit my business, so I immediately ran off and tried to figure out how to Do Art. I completely forgot that whenever God speaks to me it's an invitation to a conversation. After a few months of frustration, I finally remembered and wandered back to ask Him what He meant.

When He began speaking, He didn't even mention art. He talked about forgiving the people in my past who poked and smacked me. He mentioned blessing them was important if I wanted to live in my true home. He spoke about trusting Him for provision and about moving from a place of faith in His word to a relational trust in Jesus, the Word. And eventually, eighteen months later, I began to float upon the waves headed toward the place I belonged.

Another thing that's interesting is that jellyfish are very dangerous to their enemies. The box jellyfish explodes a most lethal venom. I think creative people are dangerous, too. They are very threatening to darkness because beauty is powerful. Perhaps we are God's plan to jeopardize evil in the world. A plan of beauty, of trust, of knowing our Heavenly Father, and expressing His light and life in a most compelling way. A plan where peace, love, and beauty are the weapons that change the world.

But we must stay off the beaches and find time to visit with our Heavenly Father about our true place in Him. And we also don't want to start poking the peculiar humans we don't understand because they may be wounded jellyfish people just like we are.

A Story of Beauty

You already know I believe God's beauty fills the earth. I also believe God's beauty fills you. His fingerprint has made you unique. No one, anywhere, is like you. No one brings to earth what you do. No one brings to life what you can.

The Call

God loves variety. Thousands of species of flowers all over the earth express beauty in very different ways. Observing flowers is a celebration of the unique and beautiful. How can I answer the question, "What is the best flower?" or "Which flower is the most beautiful?" Should I even ask that question when each flower has its own lovely essence?

God's values are different than ours. He does not compare flowers or us the way we so easily do. He does not judge us the way we judge ourselves. He values us because we are the living intention of His love. He made us. He gave each of us unique DNA, unique fingerprints, and voice waves and He has written a book for each one of us that tells a story that is ours alone. No one can live my story but me. No one can live yours but you.

God's heart is alive with love and He's longing to capture our hearts. What happens in our hearts is most important. Faith comes from the heart. What fills our hearts overflows and spills out of our mouths. What we speak brings life or death. To ourselves and to others.

I once lived in a small prairie town of 800 residents. I attended a church of 14 people. I felt

somewhat noble for my obedience to God to live in such a vast, empty land and to attend such a tiny church. One day as I worshipped, I heard God speak. "Do you know what a great honor it is for you to be with these people?" He asked me.
Obviously, I did not.

He continued speaking. He said, "These people have my ear."

And I saw how, whenever they prayed, they were heard. Families from all over the nation called when they were sick and as these simple farmers petitioned God, He answered and healing came. I was humbled seeing God's heart in a new way.

It is not how big our ministry or audience is that measures our success. Success as the world chases is not the way of Jesus. Not the way our Heavenly Father defines achievement. All of Heaven rejoices when one single soul finds Jesus. Not when I have a thousand likes on social media or 100 sales or when I've impressed the critics with my skill.

I believe there are people that no one but you can touch with your life. With your art, your craft, your writing, or your music. They will resonate to the life of God that lives in you and can be expressed only by you. No one brings Heaven to earth the way you do. No one else can show the part of God you have seen but you.

And just as natural environments are impacted when even one small bug or creature or plant becomes extinct, so are we impacted when you stop doing what God dreamed for you to do. No matter how simple or small you think it is. The world is less full and rich, less filled with His glory when you stop.

The enemy of God uses all manner of things to slow us down to keep us from living our story. He lies about the value of our work. The value of our lives. He points to others, so we will compare our work to theirs. He separates us from one another by spreading fear that we will be seen as insignificant—and maybe that is our greatest fear.

It is hard to untangle ourselves from the cultural ways of measuring our success and value, but we must. We must live in the kingdom. Rejoicing in God's garden. Filling our unique places in His glorious, diverse garden where He walks and delights in us. Where He's longing to give us His ear.

He's waiting for us to listen and live the story He's dreamed for each one of us. Don't stop. You and your work are more beautiful than you know. You matter more than you can even imagine. He's waiting for each one of us to answer His call.

My Prayer

Heavenly Father, thank you for creating me with a love for beauty and a hunger for truth. Send your Holy Spirit to guide me as I explore the spiritual environment you've designed for me. Let me rest in this place and trust you to protect me from those who don't understand people like me. Please be my protection and help me to not hurt those I don't understand. Help me understand the power of beauty and love.

Help me see myself and my gifts the way you see them. Help me value myself and others the way you do. Thank you for beauty. For artists, poets, musicians, and storytellers. For creative people who hunger for you. Bless us to live in our true home in you. In Jesus' name, amen.

You did not choose me, but I chose you

and appointed you so that you might go

and bear fruit—fruit that will last—

and so that whatever you ask in my name

the Father will give you.

John 15:16

Again Jesus spoke to them, saying,
"I am the light of the world.
Whoever follows me will not walk in darkness,
but will have the light of life."

John 8:12

4 The Road

"The closer I get,
the less I can take with me."

Pastor Bill Johnson

The Road

> Have I not commanded you? Be strong and
> courageous. Do not be frightened,
> and do not be dismayed, for the LORD
> your God is with you wherever you go.
> Joshua 1:9

When you hear the voice of Jesus across the water and decide to get out of the boat, there's only one thing you can do: keep looking at Jesus. That's it. No looking at the waves. No observing how strong the wind is blowing or contemplating the storm. None of that. We all know how that ends.

Once you're out of the boat having a miraculous faith experience with Jesus, don't look down when your brain realizes you're walking on water. Don't look down because Jesus really doesn't want you to sink. You're on the water because He enjoys hanging out with you. He likes you to have exhilarating times with Him. He likes your faith in Him that draws you close.

Following Jesus

Recently, Jesus noticed my hunger as I sat in the boat. Although He's been calling me to follow Him into the unknown for quite some time now, I just couldn't see where the path would go, so I didn't listen very well. I chewed on the idea, trying to wrap my logical mind around it, but where He was leading didn't seem to go anywhere. Then one day, Jesus reminded me of Jonah and where his disobedience took him. He reminded me of the rich young ruler who could have been one of the disciples, but turned away when asked to give what he held dear. The young ruler didn't see how he could live without the only thing he trusted.

Some years ago, God encouraged me to follow Him to a new and frightening place by talking to me about Nebuchadnezzar and reminding me if I was going to seek to build my own kingdom, it would not end well. Fear of God propelled me forward. I followed Him. I walked with Him through my fear and into a time of intimacy and beauty I never dreamed of. The journey also included meeting my husband, traveling to Europe, and discovering God's heart for me.

God is not logical when He asks for our obedience. That's what makes this a faith walk. Recently, He asked me if I truly wanted to follow Him. If I would really choose Him no matter what it cost me. It's quite easy to sit in the boat and think about wanting more of God. To claim I want to do the Bible stuff–heal the sick, raise the dead, bind up the brokenhearted, deliver people from bondage… but it's quite difficult to actually get out of the boat.

I think it takes something of Him within our hearts to lift our heads in faith and hunger and say like Peter, "If that's you, Lord, ask me to come." I wonder if Jesus would have invited him to come out on the water if Peter hadn't jumped up and essentially said, "Pick me, pick me!" As I pondered this with the Lord, I saw something new. I saw how Jesus' heart soared because of Peter's eagerness to be with Him and believe in Him. Peter saw something in Jesus that drew him beyond logic into longing and action. That's what faith looks like.

I thought about my own seeking. Do I look for ways to get out of the boat? Do I cry, "If it's you, ask me to come. Call me, Jesus, I'm ready to throw off everything to follow where I've never been before. Where it is impossible to be without you. I'm ready. Pick me. Pick me." Or do I only look for faith that makes my life more comfortable?

I finally got out of the boat. *I believe, Lord, help my unbelief.* When you get out of the boat, there's only one thing to do, keep looking at Jesus.

Obeying God

Several months ago, I woke up from a dream where Jesus walked away. Later, I could laugh, but at the time I saw myself standing in the middle of a dirt road surrounded by prairie fields as far as I could see and feeling wildly scared. I looked down at something on the ground near my feet and when I looked up all I could see was Jesus' back as he walked down the road. Away from me.

What? My mind started moving in hyper-mode. *But the Bible says He never leaves me. He is my Good Shepherd. He leads and guides me. Where is He going? Why is He going?*

And then I saw it. He **was** leading me. He expected me to follow.

I don't know why I didn't see it at first. Maybe the surge of fear delayed me or maybe I am just one of His slower children. He leads and guides, but do I follow well? Obviously, not always.

This morning, again, it felt like He wasn't here. I went through a list of things I might have done to offend Him. I wondered if there were areas of repentance I needed to address. I asked Him what I should be doing that I wasn't. I didn't hear a thing. I remembered my dream and asked God where I should be following Him.

Follow is another word for obey, although it is a more comfortable word and carries less religious baggage for me, it means the same thing. Am I following where He wants to go and doing what He wants to do or am I just standing around in the road thinking?

There is a recurring fear of lack in my life. Rearing its voice above the voice of God to speak, loudly, lies that tend to immobilize me. Lies that slow my feet until they stop altogether and I stand in the middle of the road watching Jesus walk away.

My enemy, who hates me because I am so valuable to God. Who hates me because I am made in God's image and I am loved deeply, even to the cross--that enemy hates God and all that He loves. That enemy knows how powerful the words and promises of my Heavenly Father are in my mouth. He will do anything he can, create any lie to keep me from following Jesus into the fruitful destiny God dreamed for me.

I see it is obedience that keeps me following, but wavering in my devotion to Christ slows me down and makes me a target for the smelly lies of the Evil One. His tactics never change. I should be smarter by now, but so often I just believe the wrong words.

First, my attention moves from Jesus and onto whatever is bothering me. Then my mind starts focusing on it until I no longer see the promise in God's eyes and heart and I am primed and ready to listen to the enemy when he comes to voice his prophecy and promises over my life. Promises of lack, emptiness, and failure. And yet in the faithfulness of my God, I hear the Holy Spirit whisper in my heart, "Don't listen. He's a liar."

As I take time to repent from my unbelief, from my unfaithful ways, I see Jesus ahead of me on the road, looking over His shoulder, smiling and motioning me to hurry and come on.

The Road

My Prayer

Heavenly Father, forgive me for my sin of unbelief. For not seeing how big and beautiful your plans are for me. For not seeing how awesome you are. How trustworthy. How faithful to keep me in my future and hope. Forgive me for seeing the enemy so large and powerful when you said he's not. When he was created by you and his power was destroyed at the cross.

Come, Holy Spirit of Jesus, and be strength, hope, and life in me and through me, to a world of people who know torment as I do and even more. Help me follow you well this day and every day. In Jesus' name, amen.

Stewarding Relationship

The other day God started talking about a goose and a golden egg. About how I spend my energy in life; how I sacrifice a lot of time, peace, and joy to gain something I highly value. He opened my eyes to see how I chase this golden egg, making prayers, hoping to convince God to give it to me. How I pray for protection for the egg and myself during the chase. How I believe it is my right to have the egg. To own it. Sometimes I consider it my job to chase the egg. I think, *well, God gave it to me, of course I'm responsible to make sure it doesn't get away.* I know God's trying to teach me that the gift is never more important than the Giver and never more important than spending time getting to know The One who gives me the gifts.

When I'm chasing the golden egg in my life, all my prayers begin and end with petitions for it. All my focus is on this golden orb or lack of it. Your egg may be different than mine but each of our eggs represents an area of lack in our lives. The career that isn't quite climbing. The bills that aren't quite being paid every month. The dream or project that just doesn't work right. The ministry that's floundering. Our relationships with people, our gifts, or talents. There are golden eggs in all our lives. Eggs that take our focus, that drive us down a tortured path on a quest that exhausts the fun, the joy, and the vitality of our lives.

God began speaking to me about focusing on the goose instead. He invited me to take care of the goose that laid the golden eggs. I saw I was called to nurture the source of my dreams, my abundance, and my joy. The goose is not God, but rather it represents my relationship with God. God who is the giver of all good gifts. My relationship with Him is the source of all golden eggs in my life. My invitation is to steward my relationship with The One who offers fullness and abundance. I am called to care for the gift that is His presence because everything I need is in Him. And then, through this one act of coming closer. Of opening my heart's door to Jesus so He is in me and I am in Him. He stewards the path of my egg. He makes the high places flat. He makes the crooked places straight. There is no more torment in gaining the golden egg, only joy in co-laboring with The One whose heart desires to give. The One whose heart I know and trust.

I cannot manipulate God but He longs to be with me, in relationship with me. He waits for me to notice the goose, as it were, and lift my hands from the egg to see the Living One who is the source of all. A living, breathing being who loves me so deeply He gave His most precious son as a gift to redeem me from the kingdom of darkness. From the power of the evil one whose intent is always to destroy—to drive me to distraction as he steals from me and lies to me. But God reaches out toward me with His magnificent love and longing and simply waits for me to take my eyes off the golden egg and look into His face.

We are made in the image of God and have a great capacity for accomplishing things, great reserves of strength, and strong wills to survive so the quest for the golden egg can consume us. It can lead us to give all for it—all peace, joy, hope, family bonds, time with friends, and relationship with God. We cannot chase the egg and care for the goose at the same time. It is only possible to do one or the other.

The path to leaving an egg-centered life can be a bumpy one. It takes prayer. It takes inviting Jesus into the dark places of fear within me that convinces me there isn't enough unless I have the egg. It takes faith to take my eyes off the egg when fear says it is THE most important thing in my life or tells me it is my last, best hope.

I see myself rolling a big golden egg through a tortuous path. I hear Jesus speaking behind me, inviting me, calling to me, and I hear my own voice say, "Just a minute, God, I'm doing something important here." Imagine that.

It is impossible for me to chase the egg and to love the goose at the same time. Impossible, like it is a physical impossibility for light and dark to share the same space. The nature of light causes darkness to disappear. It is impossible to do both, like Jesus told the disciples no one could serve two masters at the same time.

Following Jesus is a way of living from a paradigm that doesn't make sense but brings more life, fullness, and abundance than I ever knew was possible. The thing is, our ways are counter to God's ideas. His ways are not logical, so seekers who choose to go against all they know and understand take a giant step of faith. A step that moves the heart of God and the hands of Heaven.

Stewarding our relationship with God means taking time to know Him. Reading His word, worshiping, meditating, waiting to hear His voice. It means making time with Him a priority and it makes no sense because I have lots to do and don't really have extra time to… what, waste on God? So awful to think that way, but we do. I know it's true because until I knew Him more, I thought the same thing. And it's not like I can hide this thought from Him!

As I started getting up earlier and giving time to God, I began to hear new thoughts. Feel new feelings—like love and honor for others who had hurt me. Like confidence in God's goodness. Like hope in a future I thought I was too old to explore.

In our time together, He began to speak about my business and my writing. Creative thoughts, interesting ideas, and strategies. He gave me plans about things I had given up on, and I saw the fishermen lower their nets one more time, obeying the words of Jesus, though they had fished all night without catching a thing. I saw their excitement and amazement when the filled nets nearly sunk the boat. I heard Jesus laugh at the look on my face when I realized He meant for me to do the same thing, to launch that failed project one more time, to lower my fishing nets yet again at His word.

I cannot hear God if I am not listening. We all live busy lives. Most of our listening is done between tasks or while we're doing something else, like waiting in line at the store or weeding the garden, or driving to work. It is important to make Him a part of our lives in all those places, but it's critical to make a space for God that is His alone. One He does not share with any other task. He died so He could have a close relationship with us. It matters to Him. It must matter to us, too. If I cannot hear God, I will not know when or where to drop my nets. I won't know there's a coin hidden in a fish for my need. I won't know which fish has my coin. I won't even know there is a fish!

The source of what I need is never in answers such as a golden egg, a coin, or a fish. The source of what I need is in the questions. A searching heart that seeks for God asks, "What is on your heart today? How can I come closer? What must I do to see you?" This heart finds Him. The heart that stewards a relationship with God is a heart prepared for transformation. It's a great journey following Jesus and you want to be on it.

Directing My Focus

The world does not need one more angry person. That's me when I focus on the surrounding darkness and become offended by criminals instead of propelled by God's love for the lost. When I focus on injustice, anger rises in me instead of hope for restoration. When I look at systems embedded with chaos and lies, despair overwhelms me and I lose faith in the truth of His redemption.

I saw a picture while I was praying not long ago. It was a young boy with eyes like Superman. Eyes that shined light rays at whatever he focused on and the light made what he looked at come alive. He looked at a dead snakeskin and the snake came alive. He looked at a wilted flower in the garden and it bloomed big and beautiful with life.

No matter how lifeless things first appear, our attention makes them grow. It empowers them to live. What we focus on grows. We must choose carefully because we have power. There is no disputing that there is a dead snake in the garden, but we can deny it the power to live and divert us from life.

The Road

There are things in my peripheral vision that are threatening, fearful, or troubling, but God has been very strict with me on what I can entertain in my thoughts and vision. His word is clear on what must hold my attention. His ways are higher. He has given us power to call things that are not as if they are. To speak life into the good bits of our garden, our environment, even our friends and family. Sometimes it's easier to only see what is wrong or what the enemy is doing. Maybe it's just a habit, but there is another way, a way that brings goodness to life.

Perhaps if we're intentional in where we focus our eyes and attention, we can experience newness of life every day. We can honor each other by focusing on the good. In chaos, we can look for the one lovely thing, no matter how wilted and we can see it bloom as we watch. We can find good things in other people. See the opportunities in challenging circumstances. We can even focus on our promises from God and see them come to life.

Finally, my brothers, whatever is true,
whatever is honorable, whatever is just,
whatever is pure, whatever is lovely,
whatever is commendable,
if there is any excellence,
if there is anything worthy of praise
think about these things.

Philippians 4:8

Practicing Joy

As I followed Jesus down the road, I realized God was fun. It was a new idea for me. I did not arrive into adulthood believing life was fun, so it was quite a surprise when I felt Jesus laughing during my prayer time one day. The joy that filled the room was electric, and I finally understood the verse, "The joy of the Lord is my strength." There was power in the joy I experienced at that moment. I also realized that playing brings me closer to God. Playing is an activity God uses to create a childlike heart in me, a heart that trusts and experiences wonder.

From the early days of accepting Jesus as my savior, through years of teen angst, and finally, to a prodigal's reception of the Father's love, Jesus actually followed me and would not let me go. In recent years, my relationship with God has shifted. He speaks louder or maybe I just listen harder. He comes closer, or perhaps I simply stopped running. I don't know exactly what ignited this precious gift of His presence, but I am changed by it. I am being made childlike with a fresh trust in His goodness.

I explored the art and science of bubbles as an adult. Someone bought me a big bubble set as a gift. I think perhaps it was meant as a joke, but it captured my curiosity and delight in art. There is science in bubbles: elasticity, surface tension, chemistry, light, and even geometry. There is art in the colors and the motion and there is wondrous fun making bubbles and watching their flight.

I have become childlike in some ways. Healthy ways, I like to think, although you may disagree because as adults we are supposed to be, well, adult-like. I am not saying I abdicate my responsibilities, only that I have found a way to have joy while doing them and also to make room in my life for intentional play. This new, childlike heart opens my eyes each day to things that inspire wonder and cause me to experience God everywhere. It encourages me to keep looking for Him in all my living.

I think when we miss out on certain experiences in our childhood, like fun and the joy of our salvation, God uses play to heal us, to show us who He is, and that He is joyful and truly good. He told the disciples to let the children come to Him, then explained that for any of us to enter the kingdom, we would have to be like them. That sounds like permission to grab bubbles and practice.

To be like a child is to be given the gifts of faith, curiosity, and wonder. An understanding that God speaks not only in metaphors. He has literal plans and purposes in the stories He tells. In the pictures and dreams He gives, there is a glimmering reality. He is famous for making something from nothing. It is what He does best. He touches us with His Godness, His goodness and creates beauty from ashes, humans from dust, birds and fish with His voice. He planned and created systems in nature that have profoundly touched the curious from the beginning of time. The phenomena of river systems and watersheds, rain and clouds, oceans, and weather cycles.

The way of a child of God is the way of wonder, curiosity, seeking, and finding. The way into the Kingdom, the way of receiving the Kingdom, is coming to Jesus curious and open. Like a child approaches an iris for the first time—touching, smelling, eyeing every little flower thing closely. No fear, just wonder and curiosity. What if we approached Jesus and His kingdom that way?

What would we discover?

"Let the children come to Me;
do not hinder them,
for to such belongs the kingdom of God.
Truly, I say to you, whoever does not receive the
kingdom of God like a child shall not enter it."
And he took them in his arms
and blessed them, laying his hands on them.

Mark 10:14b-16

The Road

My Prayer

Heavenly Father, teach me about joy. Help me to be trusting, curious, and playful like a child. Jesus, come into my heart and life in the way you want to; unhindered by my preconceptions of who you are.

Let there be fun in my life. Let me live humbly so I can embrace a childlike way and enter your kingdom where Jesus is a joyful King.

Dear Lord, let me be an expression of your joy to others today. In Jesus' name, I ask these things, amen.

5 The Heart of God

Thus says the Lord who made the earth,
the Lord who formed it to establish it—
the Lord is his name:
'Call to me and I will answer you,
and tell you great and hidden things
you have not known.'

Jeremiah 33:2-3

The Heart of God

God doesn't require my goodness. He wants my heart. He wants me to turn toward Him so He can show me His goodness.

One day I was pondering the Bible verse, "Do not be overcome by evil but overcome evil with good." What would that look like in my life?

I sensed God speaking in my heart. "Goodness is who I am. Kindness is my nature. I never change and I never lie." In a moment I saw how powerful His kindness is. How hard I struggled to believe in it because it didn't make sense. Why would He be good to me on the days when I was being a brat? Snapping at my family. Hiding from cranky clients. And being generally selfish.

He doesn't change because of my actions. He just keeps looking at me with love. Handling me with gentleness. Leading me to repent with His kindness. In His light, I see the darkness in my heart. In His arms, I am transformed. Not by my work, my sweat, or my battle stance do I change, but in His presence. By His mercy. By His love. By His kindness. God is for me. He's for you. He is not against us in any way. He is against the devil in every way. But always for us. Always for love.

If we are not convinced of God's goodness or of His good heart, if we do not truly believe all His thoughts for us are good, then the words He speaks to us may be interpreted differently than He intends. We may only hear words of judgment where He intends redemption and reconciliation. Our faith for overcoming the enemy can be impacted. Our belief that God wants to fight for us. Our understanding that we are victors, not victims, may not come alive inside of us if we are still questioning God's motives.

I think God is searching the dark corners of our hearts. Getting to the roots of where our wounds and unmet needs make a space, a stronghold, for the enemy to work from. That we may truly trust and receive Jesus as bigger. Bigger than our pain. Bigger than the enemy's lies. Bigger than life on this planet.

He's going straight to where I have not abandoned myself to Him. He's exposing my greatest fears. And He's giving me truth that sets me free. In praise and thanksgiving, I offer honor to The One who not only says I am not alone, but who wraps me in loving arms of acceptance. Whose only thoughts of and for me are good. I give Him praise because He not only expresses good, but because He is always good. In my praise, He comes and I see Him and experience this truth. And I am set free from my fears. As I focus on Him in praise, I see Him destroying the works of the enemy in my life. I see God healing me on the inside so I may love Him with a whole heart.

> Fear not, for I am with you;
> be not dismayed, for I am your God.
> I will strengthen you, I will help you,
> I will uphold you with My righteous right hand.
>
> Isaiah 41:10

God's Heart for You

You are God's wildest dream. You probably didn't know that. I know I didn't. No one ever told me. Maybe they didn't know either. I have ached most of my life with an underlying sense of my own lack. A self-hatred even. Knowing I was not good enough, but fighting for a place of worth. Thinking if I worked hard enough, I could prove the voice inside was wrong. I could find rest from the driving torment. And yet believing if I got too close to God, He would surely expose and crush my being because He would see right through me to the nothing I really was.

But when He came close, He didn't do that at all. When I finally came to the end of any hope in my ability to make something good of my life and invited Him into my heart, He was not the God I'd always feared. He was a God of such immense love, such personal compassion that I realized I didn't really know Him at all. I was like one of the children of Israel following Moses into the desert. I saw God's acts occasionally in apparently random moments, but without a true understanding of how He came or why. For years, I tried to do the right things to make my spiritual life bigger, richer, and more meaningful. To make it more hopeful. Turning teachings into formulas to get my basic needs met. Working hard to keep fear, poverty, and emptiness at a distance so there would be something promising, something alive in me. Something that looked and felt like God.

I knew in the core of my being that He was real. That He was awe-inspiring. That He was beautiful. Creation had always spoken His name and reality to me. One day in all my brokenness, from a place of incredible fear and pain, I invited Him in to work in the dark places of my heart. The areas that resisted Him, that did not trust Him. I asked Him to come and bring His light and life to me.

As I opened my heart to Him, He opened His heart to me. And it is true, all His thoughts are good. All His thoughts toward me are healing, love, joy, and delight. He created the earth and all its wondrous beauty for me. For you. For us. It was for Him to have a place to walk with us and share His great Father's heart with His children. For us to explore. To discover. To learn of Him and to learn of ourselves. To dream. To build. To create and to play.

He valued us so much—each one of us with our unique fingerprints and personalities, in all our quirkiness—that He literally redeemed us by choosing to die rather than not be able to meet with us heart to heart. Jesus took all that I am not, all lack in me, all driven pain, all tormented failings so that I and you could be all that Father God dreamed us to be. He gave his life to free all that He knew was within us. To remove all barriers between us and Himself so we would know the powerful love that gives us life rich and glorious.

We are God's intention. The biggest dream He ever had. The ones He gave His all to, so He could bring us close to Him. We delight Him. Every single one of us. There is no approved method of walking with Him. Once we invite Jesus inside our hearts and meet the loving arms of our Abba Father, there is no formula. He addresses us with His Father's heart right to the place of wounding that needs love and healing most. He knows this place best because He knows us so intimately. Better than we know ourselves. His touch is gentle. His breath is soft and filled with the healing power of Heaven when He comes to meet with us.

Jesus is the perfect model of what walking with the Father looks like. His response was to always only do what the Father asked Him to do. And He obeyed perfectly. Everyone who came was healed. People with big faith. People with little faith.

People were healed in all manner of ways. By touching His clothes. By a smearing of mud and His spit. By a word He spoke. Every hungry person was filled.

Jesus said that anyone who had seen Him had seen the Father. His compassion and miracles expressed the heart of our Heavenly Father and showed us the kind of intimate relationship God wants with each one of us.

God is after our hearts. Longing to walk with us. To have conversations with us. He suffered and died for that opportunity. We are so valuable to Him. We have the highest worth of anything on the planet to our Creator, Father, God. Each unique one of us.

I am God's wildest dream. You are God's Wildest Dream. We must never forget this.

"Forgiveness is unlocking the door
to set someone free and realizing
you were the prisoner"

Max Lucado

God's Heart of Forgiveness

God consistently talks to me about forgiveness. He reminds me of people I have, intentionally, forgotten. People who hurt me or offended me. People I didn't want to remember. People I didn't want to forgive. People who made me put my hands on my hips and stamp my foot and say, "they don't deserve my forgiveness!"

To fully receive forgiveness, I must walk in forgiveness. I cannot live in the kingdom without forgiving others. I think God let me visit the kingdom so I would get a glimpse of His glorious intentions. Or maybe when I was too young to know better, He allowed me safe passage for a bit. But as I follow Jesus, He begins to speak more seriously to me. He lets me know I cannot inhabit or inherit my place in the kingdom without forgiving people. I cannot hold their sins against them. I am not allowed to withhold forgiveness. Jesus' sacrifice brought enough forgiveness into the world to cover us all. If I follow Him. If I love Him, I will see this sacrifice was enough. Enough for all my horrendous sins and all of yours. Enough for me to forgive and bless my enemies because when I was an enemy of God, He forgave me. He said, "Father, forgive her. She doesn't know what she's doing. Do not hold her sins against her. Hold them against me. Let my sacrifice be enough to make her whole, free, and alive."

Forgiving my enemies makes room in their lives for God to come in and destroy the foundations of the devil's work. It allows me to speak freedom and life and light over people, families, cities, and communities.

When I gave God permission to create a clean heart in me, when I asked, even sought Him, for a whole heart, He came in and started rooting around opening boxes and dirty little bags I didn't know were there. I have a great capacity for ignoring ugly and painful things. Whenever I am overwhelmed by them, I pretend they aren't there. I push them into a far corner of my heart and walk away. Once I've done my angry dance of unforgiveness, I never look back. Then one day Jesus came knocking on the door of my heart, wanting to come in and be closer to me. He asked to come share a meal and be friends. It was years before I trusted Him enough, before I was brave enough to let Him into the place of my hiddenness. I've come to see that while I was ignoring painful and ugly things, fear nibbled at the edges and made me ignore God's call as well.

Jesus stands at the door of the hearts of his followers. He knocks on the door of those of us who've said, Yes, at some time in our lives. He patiently waits to be invited inside. Waits for us to choose Him and to bravely open the door.

Into God's Heart of Forgiveness

Following Jesus into forgiveness is a big thing. As a model for walking in love, Jesus was pretty much unrivaled. I can hear Him saying, "Forgive them, Father, for they know not what they do," as they ended His life that day.

On most days, I am not like Jesus.

Heavenly Father, forgive my dark heart that does not want forgiveness for my enemies but wants to call down fire upon them instead. That wants to see them pay for their sins against me. My dark heart that desires vengeance for the pain they brought into my life.

And I see Jesus not raising a sound against those persecuting Him, spitting on Him, wounding Him, and bringing Him great mockery and pain.

I hear Him say, "No one takes my life. I freely give it."

I see His heart, His trust in His Father's intentions. His trust that the future of His obedience is glorious because He knows His Father's heart toward Him. And He knows if there had been any other way to forgive the world, Jesus would have been spared the cross.

As Jesus hung on the cross, He forgave all those who had put Him there. He asked the Father to forgive them, too. I believe it was because He saw the Father's heart for those created in His image. Those He wanted to call sons and daughters. Those He longed to hear cry, "Abba, Father." Out of God's great love, forgiveness was born and redemption came alive.

As He forgave us, as He released our sins from us, so we are to do likewise. To share in the sufferings of Christ is, perhaps, to die to my heart of vengeance. To fall in love with the Father and want

His kindness that leads to repentance to be experienced by those I see as my enemies.

...bless them that curse you, do good to them that hate you, and pray for them which despitefully use you, and persecute you. Matthew 5:44 (KJV)

This is bigger than 'committing them to God in prayer' because praying those words still feels like permission to hold on to a dark little part of me that wants them to get what's coming to them. Thinking, *surely my prayer will help God discipline or punish them for what they've done.*

When I bless my enemies, I must come to God with an open heart and open hands, asking Him to richly pour out His love upon them. Asking Him to pour out His mercy, hope, grace, and goodness upon those who brought the greatest pain into my experience. Only then do I understand the heart of God, who wants no one to perish. Who showers goodwill on all. Whose forgiveness covers the whole earth.

To follow Jesus, I must forgive. The way of Jesus is a path of continual forgiveness of my sins. Of the sins of others. The way of Jesus leads to life. To freedom from carrying the burden of others' sins. God cares deeply about our wounds. We are precious to Him. He gathers our tears in bottles, but He doesn't see my enemy as an enemy. It is not His goodness in me that cries out for vengeance and judgment on the ones who hurt me. It is my anger. It is the voice of my pain and injustice crying out to be heard. To be seen. To be vindicated.

Am I not willing to take the hurt and give it to God so another can be set free from the flames of hell? Set free from the torment of the true enemy of God, the devil, and his lies? So another could be led to repentance by the kindness of God in me and through me? Or must I demand every last coin owed from the one who wounded me? Am I choosing not to walk into the glory before me but stay in the shadow of the earthly realm where an eye for an eye rules?

The way of Jesus demands purity of heart. At some point, He shows me what I can't take into the kingdom. Things I carry that don't fit through the door. Things that bring death, not life. With forgiveness, I touch the heart of God and I become the heart of God to others.

My Prayer

Heavenly Father, help me be a person who forgives. A person of patience, hope, and compassion. A living testimony of your love.

Show me how to pray for all people, so your compassion and kindness comes to them. Help me be a person of reconciliation introducing others to Jesus. To their Heavenly Father.

Father, forgive those who hurt me. Please don't hold their sins against them. They don't know what they've done. Forgive me for holding onto their sins. For demanding they pay when Jesus has already paid the price for all our sins.

Give me a heart for all those You love, but I don't. The ones who frighten me, who hurt me, who criticize, and misjudge me. The ones who accuse me, even of things I never did. The ones who throw rocks because they don't understand me. The ones who mock me because it's easier than getting to know me.

Help me, Father, to stay nestled in your heart, feeling the beat of your love for all. Help my heart to beat that way, too. In Jesus' name, I ask these things, amen.

God's Heart in the Dark

One morning, the Lord spoke to me about my default position in a crisis. He let me know that what I choose is very, very important.

When I look into the eyes of Jesus, I understand who I am. I experience love and acceptance. He gives me a revelation of how greatly He values me. How treasured I am. He makes me alive. His life fills me with love, light, hope, and joy. I don't get that when I look in the mirror. I only see what's wrong, what's missing, and what's broken.

When I come to Him, He does not show me what's wrong or missing. He simply begins to fill me with Himself and there is nothing wrong or missing or broken in Him. He shows me I am the righteousness of God in Christ Jesus. He gives me beauty for my ashes. The oil of joy for my sadness.

When I come to Him in prayer for you, He does not show me what's wrong or missing or broken in you, either. He shows me His great joy and delight in you. He shows me His heart that is huge with love for you. He shows me His great faith that you will come closer, with a whole heart, to know Him.

His love believes all things. There is faith in God. He planted it in us. His faith that we would respond to Him is what led Jesus to the cross. His compelling love is why Jesus laid down His life so the Father would have His heart's delight, which is us. For God so loved the world that He gave His one and only son.

When I'm challenged in my life, when darkness suddenly surrounds me, my default response is to search my heart, listing my failures, recounting my sins, seeking my place of repentance. I cannot see God's heart. I do not remember His word about me or my situation. I cannot feel His love. Condemnation and confusion become my food. In a crisis, I rarely see His heart for others. Usually, strife and frustration come into my relationships. Peace and joy flee. This position of looking to myself, leaning on my strength or understanding, is not God's way for me when I am in trouble.

My other default in a crisis is to look for an enemy. I begin looking for what the enemy is doing in my life. Questioning, searching him out, focusing on him instead of Jesus. Stepping off the narrow path of God's leading, I venture into a murky, smelly swamp looking for the evil force I know is hiding to ambush me. I think if I can identify him, I can conquer him. Shushing God when He tries to get my attention, saying, "Just a minute, can't you see I'm busy here? I'll be right with you," as I continue my quest for understanding the dark swamp.

Neither one of these responses leads to life. The only response I should ever have is to run into my Heavenly Father's arms. To seek Jesus. To wait for the still, small voice to speak to me. Because I cannot know He's working in me through the crisis if I do not go to Him. Sometimes He wants to teach me strategy. Sometimes it's faith and patience. Sometimes it's to reveal how big and good He is. Or to show me how much authority I have in Jesus. And sometimes He wants to tell me something about Himself I never even dreamed of before. Something beyond my understanding that overpowers the darkness.

So many times I forget that everything in my life is an invitation to a conversation with God. He waits for me to show up. To confirm I'm choosing Him. To reveal my heart is focused on His heart and that He matters to me. That I will listen. I will wait humbly before Him for power from on high. The Father sees in the darkness, so I don't really need to. I simply need to listen for Him to tell me what I'm to do. What I'm to resist. What I'm to cast out. Where I need to repent. Where I need to worship.

I can only get what I need from spending time with God. His answers are bigger than what's inside of me. He is of Heaven and I have no frame of reference for what's in Him. I can only see it when I ask, seek, and knock. My need is a temporary affliction. His answer builds a permanent, unshakable foundation under my feet. I have to turn the care of my crisis over to Him before I can let my curiosity loose to follow His voice. When I seek to see Him, staring down the narrow path, I look up and He's there. When I see Him, I see everything I need, every single thing is in Him. HE is what I need. And He lives in me.

My Prayer

Heavenly Father, help me to seek you first, in the midst of all my everyday challenges. Help me to see Jesus in my daily life and to see I am wrapped in the comfort and confidence of the Holy Spirit who lives within me.

Please open the eyes of my heart so I can see things the way you do. So I can experience the victory, the wholeness, and the peace you've planned for me instead of defeat, brokenness, and fear.

Dear Lord, help me follow you faithfully and hopefully into the future you've dreamed for me. Help me to see I am loved dearly. Grow my desire and ability to love you more. In Jesus' name, I ask these things, amen.

I leave you with a blessing for your journey.

BLESSING*

In the name of Jesus, I bless you with God's comfort around you and sinking deep into your heart. I bless you with rest and peace from your Heavenly Father so you may know He is for you, always. That He is present with you, always. I bless you with an understanding of God's delight in you. And an understanding of His joy in being with you.

I bless you, in the name of Jesus, that The Lord would be strength for you in your weakness. That God's grace would carry you into trusting Him fully in the dark and in the pain. I bless you to experience His presence and love that always surrounds you.

In Jesus' name, I bless you with a revelation of Jesus, the mighty King, the host of heaven's armies, and His heart to defend you. I bless you with the power of the name of Jesus rising for you against any plan of the enemy that tries to affect your destiny.

I bless you to know God's blessings for you and the ones you love. I bless you that God's face would shine upon you today and always, in Jesus' name.

*Inspired by *The Way of Blessing* by Rod Godwin

The Heart of God

About the Author

Life is incredibly hard when you are born sensitive. Apparently, voices are louder, colors are brighter, and arguments are more troubling to us than the average, more resilient, population. We are the artists, poets, musicians, and writers. The photographers, storytellers, and crazy ones. What I found most disconcerting was my inability to make anyone else understand what I saw or felt.

We are easily broken, but most of us, weary of communication that falls short of connection, simply raise walls and stay safely behind them. Not that my parents didn't try to help but without a frame of reference, something like a duck-billed platypus in a family of minks is an oddity and the worst kind of trouble for young parents.

I learned to build walls early on, so although I was not flexible enough to be resilient, I was surrounded by thick, protective walls. Until one day, God showed up at the gate. My blogs and books are the stories of what happened next.

I was a late blooming graduate of Oregon State University where younger students called me Mom. I've had three careers in my lifetime and would love to add author as my final dream job.

My first career in retail management lasted around fifteen years. I spent another fourteen years working in community and economic development. For the last two decades, I've been building websites, creating graphics, and writing every chance I get.

Thank You

Thank you for taking time to read *Journey of a Broken Seeker*, the first book of my series, A Seeker's Heart.

If you're on the journey, too, come on over to my readers' page for additional resources and free downloads.

If you join my list you'll be the first to know when I launch new books, have new resources, or when my books are on sale.

May God bless you on your journey!

www.godswildestdream.com/readers/

www.ingramcontent.com/pod-product-compliance
Lightning Source LLC
Chambersburg PA
CBHW020428010526
44118CB00010B/482